1595

■■■■■ C O N T

KU-305-862

Contents

Dedication

To J W H Life

For his unstinting support.

Success in business derives from getting, keeping and using competitive advantage. Branding is the most powerful way to do this. The world's biggest brands belong to the world's most profitable companies.

Brand marketing is centuries old and began when businesses that had established a reputation in the market added a brand mark to their products to distinguish them from competitors' products.

Today, brands can be companies, products or services. For simplicity, this book refers to corporate brands. If you are working with a product or service brand, the generic principles are the same the main differences arise in the marketing mix.

Brands offer compelling benefits over and above conventional marketing:

- Brands support premium pricing on high volumes, creating improved sales and profit margins.

Building a Brand

in a week

PETE LAVER

Hodder & Stoughton

A MEMBER OF THE HODDER HEADLINE GROUP

Orders: please contact Bookpoint Ltd, 130 Milton Park, Abingdon, Oxon
OX14 4SB.
Telephone: (44) 01235 827720, Fax: (44) 01235 400454. Lines are open from
9.00–6.00, Monday to Saturday, with a 24 hour message answering service.
Email address: orders@bookpoint.co.uk

British Library Cataloguing in Publication Data
A catalogue record for this title is available from The British Library

ISBN 0 340 859 016

First published 2002
Impression number   10 9 8 7 6 5 4 3 2 1
Year   2007 2006 2005 2004 2003 2002

Typeset by SX Composing DTP, Rayleigh, Essex.
Printed in Great Britain for Hodder & Stoughton Educational, a division of
Hodder Headline Plc, 338 Euston Road, London NW1 3BH. by
Cox & Wyman Ltd, Reading, Berkshire.

- Brands are one of the few investments that do not wear out. In fact, the older they get, the stronger they get. The high prices paid for brands reflect the long-term return in shareholder value. Brands capture investment, reducing risk.
- Strong brands compete on price and quality and they compete in the third dimension of intangible brand equity. This encourages innovative marketing and results in strong, differentiated markets.
- Brands own a place in the minds of their customers (the only advertising space worth paying for) and have an astonishing resistance to change. Lowenbrau and Stella Artois beers both date from the middle ages and have outlasted civilisations.
- Brands support and defend innovation. Lycra was quickly copied as a product, but customers want Lycra. The brand defends itself and, in addition, can be legally protected.
- Brands segment the market and create options for growth through extension and brand families. Developing a brand is much less risky than starting again.
- Brands are surprisingly resilient in the face of mismanagement!

Much lip-service is paid to brands, but few of us treat them with the respect they require if they are to deliver their full potential. Building a successful brand is what this book is about. Achieving this task in a competitive environment is a challenge, yet it is achievable. Over the next seven days you will be guided through the processes of building a brand from first principles and growing its equity in the short and long term.

It's great fun, so let's get started.

From products to brands

- What brands are and how to use them
- The benefits of branding and the brand building process

The brand building process

Four crucial questions must be answered powerfully and effectively to achieve a winning brand strategy. Can you answer them for your business?

1 What is your business for – what is its essence?
2 How do you define and segment your customers?
3 What differences exist between your business and those of your competitors and how do you capitalise upon these differences?
4 Which channels to market are most beneficial to you and do they form the focus of your business activity?

The questions seem simple and yet most of us find it extremely difficult to provide clear, precise answers. The answers are essential, however, because they form the foundation of a successful brand plan. Keep your initial answers and see how they have changed by the end of today.

There are five outputs of the brand planning process:

1 4C analysis (company, customers, competitors, channels)
2 Positioning
3 Growth vectors
4 Growth drivers
5 Action

4C analysis

4C analysis (the name is taken from the first letter of each key field – company, customers, competitors, channels) guides you, step by step, through your strategic analysis and creates the opportunity to achieve your all-important competitive advantage.

- *The company*: the company or brand audit will develop the anatomy of the brand and its equities. What the business stands for, its unique essence, will emerge from this and lead to an understanding of what the brand should be telling its audience.
- *The customers*: traditional segmentation methods target customers and prospective customers without any discrimination between the two (mention this to anyone involved in sales and be prepared to duck!). In contrast, 4C analysis guides you to a complete customer map, taking these vital components into account. The analysis will identify the most suitable customers to target for the brand. At this point you will know what to say and with whom you will initiate the discussion. The output from this piece of work will define your customers precisely in terms of what they need. You will also have a measurement of customer loyalty; the driving force behind profitability.
- *The competitors*: we choose our competitors as surely as we choose our customers. You will need to make an industry model based on the needs you serve and competitors who meet similar needs. The output of your work in this field will be a clear view of the specific differences between your business and those of key competitors expressed as a competitor map. Exploiting these differences reveals your competitive advantage.

- *The channels*: there are many means by which the brand's products and services can reach its customers. These include retail and wholesale outlets, the internet and direct mail. But brands are known by the company they keep. To be in the wrong company sends out the wrong signals. This part of the process involves mapping available and potential channels to market in terms of current and future potential.

Positioning

Effective positioning focuses your brand in the eyes of consumers, precisely where you want it in relation to your competitors. In other words, it highlights your point of difference and creates competitive advantage. Using the data collected from 4C analysis, you refine your brand map to select the most relevant message to communicate. Your customer analysis provides the data to select your primary audience. Your competitor analysis enables you to select the most appropriate competitor against which you are capable of establishing a significant point of difference. Finally, channel analysis leads to the selection of the most appropriate trade marketing channels.

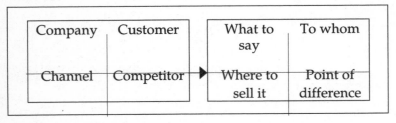

Figure 1 Distilling data from 4C analysis to create a
positioning statement

The situational report, derived from 4C analysis, defining the essence and components of the brand. This will inform all the creative work on the brand from now on and ensure consistency over the long term.

Growth vectors

There are only a limited number of directions (vectors) that any business can follow in order to achieve growth. Essentially, you can sell more, put up the price or find a combination of the two. You need to evaluate each potential option in turn, relative to the current position, and select the best route forward.

Growth drivers

Tactical alignment of the brand plan lines up behind a clear positioning, like shoppers forming an orderly queue. For example, an exclusive, expensive market position implies high specification products at premium prices sold through exclusive outlets and advertised in top quality magazines. The traditional 4Ps approach to building a marketing mix can be very restrictive. This refers to product, place, price, promotion – key drivers of success could be reduced queues, better packaging, stronger relationships with important customers and so on. Instead, you can look at each element of the marketing mix and rank them in order of importance to your customers. In so doing, you will flesh out the drivers of success for your brand and align them to match your strategic initiatives. Finally, you can create a 'tracker' to check and measure performance. Overall, the process is seamless and effective and the tracker adds the feedback loop so that you can learn and benefit from successes (and set-backs).

Action

Finally, the plan can be put to work. The positioning, strategies and aligned mix can be worked into a project plan to drive the brand forward. Using sales and market data and the brand tracker provides feedback mechanisms to help you keep the business in control.

However complicated your business may be, this proven process ensures that the answers are clear, direct and simple for each question. Great ideas can only come from clearly setting out the issues and pinpointing clear achievable outcomes.

Understanding your brand

The first stage of 4C analysis sets out to understand and map the identity of your brand. Before starting, take a moment to understand the definition of what a brand is, before moving on to brand identity and image.

What precisely is a brand?

At the most basic level a brand is described as a name, a symbol or a sign that denotes ownership. Today, some of these symbols and signs are worth billions of dollars in recognition of the profits that will probably accrue to their owners.

Definition

A brand can be defined as a reputation in the market which has an identity (the source of the brand) which has been translated into an image (customer perception) that confers competitive value in additional sales or premium prices or both.

A brand is capable of being much more than a trademark. A brand lives inside its customers' minds and forms a shared set of beliefs within that group. A shared belief or paradigm is astonishingly tenacious and provides competitive advantages of enormous value. The best brands take on some of the aspects of a human personality. They become an invisible friend: 'My mate Marmite', for example.

The brand identity and image

Identity comes from inside the business, not from the customers. A clear understanding of the identity of your brand will ensure its consistency. Later on you will repeat this exercise, this time asking your customers in order to identify your brand image. The differences between identity and image comprise the strategic gap. Your aim is to retain the identity by adjusting the image and never the other way around.

> The image of a brand is what the audiences of the brand (customers, suppliers, potential customers, etc.) believe now. This may be true or not true and it may be good or bad. The identity of a brand is what it really is and aspires to be. Being unduly influenced by image is a mistake for a person or a brand. The finest people and the best brands have a set of values and beliefs that are not for sale and not liable to change easily. For a brand or organisation, this bedrock of principle is the anchor that holds its identity together and helps it to resist what is sometimes called strategic drift. Image is a vital concern but the direction of change and its management should almost always be towards changing the image of the brand, not its identity.

A downed pilot was being interrogated by his captors. 'What is your mission?' they barked. With pride he immediately responded, 'Our mission is to provide unfailing commitment to aerial bombardment technology with total focus on accuracy, quality and maximum damage at minimum cost.'

Mission statements are a corporate ego massage – forget them. A corporate or brand identity statement will describe the purpose of the business (its essence) and how it should be perceived and behave. Add a sensible list of company policies and the job is done.

Your brand can be understood by building a brand identity map (Figure 2) starting from its inner core (essence) and moving outwards towards its attributes (properties and appearance) and behaviour.

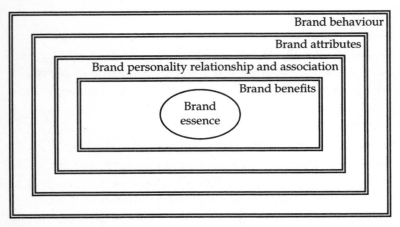

Figure 2 The brand identity map

Identity maps are atomic in structure. At the nucleus are the core values and purpose, which attract the other attributes into orbit around them. The core is resistant to change, while the attributes toward the edges need to change incrementally with the times. The map should contain only attributes (sometimes called equities) which can be understood and used strategically. Finally, the map should present the holistic face of the brand. It should be recognisable as an entity that can be understood and worked with. There is nothing wrong with a little imaginative moonshine in the identity map, provided you can sustain it. Many brand reputations are built around a good story even though it does not withstand much scrutiny. River Island is an example of a romantic brand that invites the consumer to share the fantasy. Clothing for extreme conditions would probably be a step too far for them, however, and best left to Berghaus.

Let's look at each element of a brand identity map.

The brand essence or core
The essence or core values of strong brands stand for something and communicate powerfully to people who share or aspire to similar values. The brand is a signature rather than a product or service. Aristotle said, 'If an axe had a soul its soul would be cutting.' Similarly, the invisible presence of a brand resides inside its products. The soul of the brand is its essence. People who wish to be cool may identify with and buy Virgin or FCUK. The brand's essence communicates directly to its audience by hooking into similar values. For instance, a damaged Rolex is not so valuable as a perfect example, but it is still worth much more than a fake. A damaged Rolex retains its soul; a fake never had one.

Answer the following questions to determine the values of your brand:

- What does your business do?
- What does it value?
- What would you like to hear people say about it?
- Does your business have a standpoint – something it believes in above everything else?
- Does it have a heritage?
- What story does it have to tell?

Brand needs

Human needs are functional, social and psychological. Our most important needs are functional, such as food and shelter, but once these needs are met social and psychological needs take priority. Social needs reflect the strong desires of most of us to belong and be accepted by others. Psychological needs are inner-directed and egotistical, for example, wanting to be at peace with ourselves or to achieve our potential. The extraordinary power of branding is its ability to associate with these desires and to build relationships with customers.

For instance, if you were marketing a professional football club, the needs that create the desire to attend the matches might be identified as follows:

Need category	Need
Functional needs	Food, drink, comfort, warmth, security – crowd control, entry and exit arrangements
Social needs	Tribalism, hospitality, community, competitive association with success, access to the stars
Psychological needs	Hero worship, touching the dream, excitement, entertainment, joy

Each set of needs requires a marketing solution, but some elements will be more important than others. Traditional fans will be more interested in the tribal and community elements, while less committed fans will be driven more by excitement and entertainment. Corporate clients will put hospitality at the top of their agenda, but the children will go for hero worship. Football may be the product, but motivation is the selling point.

- What needs does your brand serve?
- Are these needs predominately functional, social or psychological?
- Make a list of these needs.

Brand benefits

Human needs are met by brand benefits and not product features. One important need within most of us is to define and improve our self-concept. Our self-concept is multifaceted. For example, it includes what we think about ourselves and also what we think others think about us. Many of us will make choices based upon our self-concept in terms of how we wish to be perceived or in terms of how we think others perceive us.

Reflect a moment on these two stories.

Story 1

The wind whipped over the bonnet of the Porsche causing him to pull up the collar of his Armani jacket. Sweeping to a halt outside the Dorchester he caught the aroma of Chanel No. 5 as he opened her door. Pausing to offer her a Pall Mall and lighting one himself, he led the way inside where he ordered a bottle of Heinseck. He reflected wryly that the champagne was worth it just to see her voluptuous figure in her new Versace dress.

Story 2

The wind whipped over the bonnet of the Astra Coupé causing him to pull up the collar of his Marks & Spencer leather jacket. Sweeping to a halt outside the Crown he enjoyed the aromatic mixture of Charlie and leather as he opened her door. Pausing to offer her a Camel and lighting one himself, he led the way inside where he ordered Fosters Lager. He reflected wryly that the drinks were worth it just to see her lovely figure in her new Gap dress.

What were your perceptions of the characters in both versions of the story?

The only change between the two stories is the brands used, but our perception of the characters changes radically. Brands address social needs by saying something about their users. They also address psychological needs by delivering the feel good factor. A designer label on the inside of a jacket helps the owner to value him or herself that much more.

- **What benefits does your brand deliver to meet each need that you have identified?**

Brand relationship
'Anyone who has a relationship with a bar of soap or a can of soup is either deluded or leading a sad life!' I believe that this viewpoint is entirely understandable, but incorrect.

Marshall McLuhan (who was Director of the Center for Culture and Technology, University of Toronto) points out that many products are, in effect, extensions of human beings. A trowel is an extension of the hand. The human hand, although clever, can dig a hole more effectively with a trowel. The addition of a spade creates an even larger hole and mechanical earthmovers can create tremendous holes. Each product extends the hand to do a different task of increasing size and complexity. Similarly, a car extends the foot and a computer enhances the functions of the brain. Some products are intensely personal, such as body lotions, and others very public, such as aeroplanes. However, they all extend human potential by extension of our natural capabilities. It is not surprising that we regard many brands with affection, considering the enormous gains in performance or pleasure that they offer.

Brand personality

Unconsciously, we humanise brands with human descriptions. This habit (anthropomorphism) is a vital aspect of branding.

When a lifstyle brand announces, 'I hate school', it identifies closely with a young market who feel the same themselves. Kodak is perceived as mature and responsible while Coca Cola is young. Chanel is a sophisticated woman and Levi is a rebel.

What is the personality of your brand? To discover this ask yourself some interesting questions, for example:

- If your brand was a person who would it be?
- If your brand held a party would you go?
- If your brand had a hobby, what would it choose?

Make a note of your instinctive responses.

Brand association

When we think of a strong brand, like Virgin, our mind conjures up not only the name or trademark but also a host of other associations. These may not always be at the front of our consciousness, but we can recall them when asked. We might, for example, associate the brand with usage occasion (e.g. cereal for breakfast, champagne for celebrations) and the types of people who use it.

People asked to imagine famous people climbing aboard a Virgin aircraft visualised pop stars, footballers and supermodels. A similar exercise with BA produced the names of politicians and similar worthies. Unlike these two examples, brand associations are not always favourable. In either case, this is essential information for your analysis.

- Think of a brand you know well and list the thoughts and associations that come to mind. Do the same with your own brand and make a note of the results.

Brand attributes

Brand attributes consist of the audio and visual signatures that signal the presence of the brand.

The Nike 'swoosh' and the Direct Line jingle and phone are examples. Some brands are associated with colours, such as Body Shop's dark green. The BMW propeller badge and twin-radiators act as signatures that ratify and endorse the brand. They signal authenticity, consistency and quality.

- What are the audio and visual signatures of your brand?

Brand behaviour

Consistency is the key to effective branding. Lowenbrau was introduced in AD 1386 and is still here today. Rowntrees Fruit Pastilles were introduced in 1888. Brands offer a promise of quality and act as a beacon of consistency in a world of change. Marks & Spencer, Mars and Clerical & Medical Insurance are amongst the old, heritage brands that remain market leaders 100 years or more after their introduction.

Brands need to be consistent and to offer something that is perceived by their customers as superior to their rivals. They offer zero protection to shoddy products and services. Research shows that the big brands are more trusted than the church or the government. Abuse this trust and your brand dies.

- How does your brand behave in relation to the values you identified earlier. Keep the results for later use.

Summary

- You have looked at the astounding benefits of branding and started to think about how to exploit some of these for yourself.
- You have learned the overall structure of the brand planning process and made a start on creating your own brand identity.
- The future started today.

What have we got?

- Auditing the company and its customers
- Auditing the brand and uncovering its value

Profiling the brand

4C analysis quick review
4C analysis audits your brand and provides organised data that feeds directly into a brand proposition. On completion of each of the four stages of the analysis, you can prepare a straightforward chart specifying the conclusions reached. This consists of a brand identity map, a customer map, a competitor map and a channel plan. You have already begun the process by identifying some of the important elements of your brand's identity.

Building your own brand identity map

Using the map structure outlined on Sunday, you can begin to illustrate your brand identity as a recognisable entity. The brand identity map is a useful container to capture the information collected earlier. It pulls the data together into a holistic framework. On completion, the face of your brand will be revealed.

The starting point is to work through the thoughts and ideas you have collected and to summarise the main points down to a phrase or even a single word. Decide which category each item fits, with reference to the brand identity map (page 12) then enter it on to the map. The result may be very cluttered or very bare, depending on how you have got on so far. It is possible that you have discovered some important ideas that do not fit anywhere (the diversity of businesses is vast), in which case it may be necessary to create a new category on your map. The process is much more of an art than a science.

The example shown below presents a view of the BMW brand in the UK and goes a fair way towards explaining its success. The map for BMW suggests a unique standpoint of mechanical perfection that, coupled with its slightly younger image, has made the Ultimate Driving Machine one of the most successful brand identity programmes ever undertaken. At the core is cold precision. People rarely appear in its advertising. Its core values of thoughtful technology, performance and exclusivity are delivered through its tone of voice. Its German origin is important.

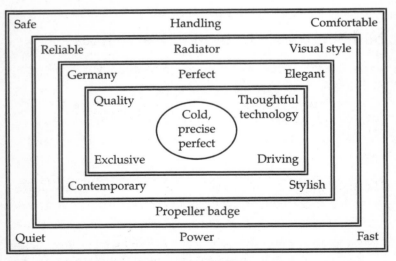

Figure 3 Brand identity map for BMW

The BMW example (a personal interpretation) displays innovation and imagination, while remaining far-sighted and deliverable. A strong identity will not excuse poor products, but it will distinguish good ones.

It is often pointed out that the distinctions between categories can sometimes be hard to define. The important point is that the model has a definite structure from the fixed core in the centre, to the more readily changeable attributes towards the outside. The categories are a crucial guide to help you to construct your map.

Using the data collected from your brand on Sunday, complete your own brand identity map. You are seeking clues about what makes your brand distinctive and different from competitors' brands. It may seem that the answers will be obvious, but this is rarely the case. The guiding principle is to create a harmonious pattern with the selected equities complementing each other. The result should be a recognisable entity. Its attributes and personality should be present on the map and should be supportable.

Benefits of the brand identity mapping process

The first benefit of the mapping process lies primarily in its ability to provide a holistic overview. The face of the brand will be looking out at you.

The second benefit lies in the descriptors you identify. Every one of them is a brand equity as valuable as any other major asset and much more valuable than most. Symbols and signs such as the Coca Cola Corporation bottle and IBM's logo are literally priceless. The fact that WHSmith and Boots the Chemist are trusted is almost certainly more valuable to those companies than any owned, physical asset. The most relevant equities in your business for today's marketplace will be used to develop your corporate strategy.

The brand identity statement

The final stage is to create the brand identity statement. This document will lay out the brand identity, adding several elements that were not covered in the visual map. This is the anatomy of the brand, enabling everyone who works with it to understand its value and purpose. It provides a template to ensure that the brand's consistency, core values and purpose are maintained and protected. It will be used to set strategy and to advise staff and creative agencies about how to treat the brand. It should be protected because it is the brand blueprint and will outlast its creator. The table below sets out the areas to be covered, although you may wish to write it out in plain text.

The Brand Identity Statement	
Name	**Content**
1 The business purpose	What the brand is for.
2 Core values	The essential nature of the brand.
3 Benefit statement	The functional, social and psychological benefits of the brand.
4 Personality	Young, old, male, female, sophisticated and clever or rugged and action-oriented. Reliable, trusted, independent.

5 Auditory and visual identity	The brand attributes including symbols, signs, colours, jingles, straplines, smells, taste, shape, form.
6 The knowledge base	What the brand can do – its skills and therefore its operational zone, including brand extensions.
7 Development	Developments, including future brand extensions.
8 Tone of voice	Who it is and how it speaks. Friendly, man to man, woman to woman, boy to girl. Its relationship with its audience.
9 Portfolio position	If there are other brands involved, how are they related, e.g. Nescafé and Gold Blend. How do their activities complement one another without getting in each other's way?
10 Image	The significant differences between this identity and the actual image of the brand with its customers. This difference is your gap analysis. You now know what you need to do to bring the image in line.
11 Behaviour	Unique ways in which the brand operates.
12 Other	Any other significant points.
13 Category and key competitors	What categories it operates in and who its main competitors are at present.
14 Numerical data	Sales and profitability. Budgets and forecasts. Market share.
15 Ratios	Return on net assets, asset utilisation, return on sales.

The brand book

Many brands develop the identity statement into a largish document, including the visual identity (logos, fonts, colour schemes, document layouts, etc). Be careful not to put your creative people in a strait-jacket. The addition of a mood board showing colour schemes, the preferred font and any brand icons (characters, logos, straplines) may well be sufficient to ensure consistency. One cigarette brand uses a mock cigarette pack with cards inside to outline the main design points.

Using the brand map, complete a brand identity statement (shown in the table above). There are a number of additional points that do not fit neatly into the map, which have been explained. Perhaps the most important is tone of voice. It is essential that the brand speaks consistently to its audience, which means understanding its relationship towards them. For example, it could be a man with a Manchester accent who talks man to man with an element of humour. The brand knowledge base explains what the brand audience think the brand can do and therefore creates a boundary in terms of the type of products or services the brand can sell.

- Can you describe the identity from the statement in a way that any ordinary person can appreciate?
- Does every word mean something valuable?
- Just as a complete personal identity card would contain a picture of the holder, so the map is the brand portrait. When you look at it do you see an entity you can understand and work with?
- Are there image gaps to be addressed? How will you address these?

Profiling the brand audience

The customer franchise

All customers are not equal. Some are worth much more than others and prospects (potential customers) are not even customers yet. All too often marketing fails to make a clear distinction between customers and prospects. The brand identity is linked to its loyal customer base. The customers who buy from it comprise its real brand equity. A store chain that attracts 1 million customers a week has a 1 million customer head start on one that is about to open.

Customer analysis

Modern consumers and business customers are streetwise. Intensive advertising and promotions have taught us to look for deals. Many businesses are learning the hard way that unselective recruitment of prospects is poor business. They take the deal and walk away. In this climate a customer strategy is vital. The solution is a good quality database that has the potential to reduce the complexity of big customer bases to a new version of the village shop. In a good village shop, big customers and regulars are given priority and shortages passed on to occasional customers and passing nomads. Loyalty is rewarded and promiscuous custom is welcomed, but never at the expense of more important customers. The shopkeeper's priorities are first to hold what he has (low churn rate) and second to sell more to his regular customers (share of wallet). He or she will know the value of regular customers (lifetime residual value).

In a typical customer analysis, 20 per cent of customers account for 60 per cent of sales and 50 per cent account for 10 per cent of sales. Few businesses can afford to ignore the 20 percent, but many do. In fact, many businesses ignore them all and focus their effort on converting prospects, i.e. winning new business.

Repeat purchase rates vary enormously across business sectors and therefore loyalty will not be a major factor for some businesses. For most, where loyalty is an important consideration, the top 20 percent require special attention. Careful profiling will draw a picture of what these people (or businesses) are like and will enable you to search for more like them. It is important to hold on to the bread and butter customers too. Many are probably unprofitable, but they will be contributing to costs. Consequently, getting rid of them is usually a bad idea – just avoid giving them too much attention.

Golden rule
The most important customers are the ones you already have. They provide your income and your brand lives in their minds. By providing existing customers with great service you enable them to tell others about you. Word of mouth builds brands.

Review your database management:

- What systems do you have in place for recording and analysing transactions?
- Do your systems provide customer data of sufficient quality?
- If no, what can you do to change this?
- How well do you know your customers?

Segmentation

It has been said that the current era will be the age of one-to-one marketing. It is certainly true that the one-to-one approach is increasing in importance, yet a sensible view takes account of larger groupings. When one message serves its purpose for an entire group, it is pointless and expensive to contact them individually.

The huge disparity between what businesses claim they can do with direct one to one marketing and the pitiful results usually achieved is amazing.

Segmentation should aim to discover and describe the needs of customers by identifying the different packages of motivators that exist within them. Only then can products be prepared to meet these requirements effectively. Segmentation is, therefore, fundamental to business strategy. It provides the information that leads directly into product and channel selection and effective communications.

The low-cost option is to treat everyone the same, but in today's overcrowded markets it is unlikely to be a viable approach for many. If there is a range of needs, you need a different approach for each.

Benefits of segmentation

- Segmentation continues a process that starts with what the business has been created to do and matches this to a precise evaluation of what customers need
- It evaluates how these needs create the market
- It describes the differences in these wants, creating segments that we know and enjoy working with

- It starts a process capable of recognising and rewarding loyalty
- It measures and prioritises these segments, putting them at the heart of the business, so that product, channel and communication strategy can be built around them
- It develops a process for organic growth based on understanding and keeping and recruiting loyal customers
- It leads to the prioritisation and selection of segments and to positioning the brand

Stage 1: identifying the market

Take some time to consider what the future might look like for your business. What will have changed five years from now? Ten years from now? What changes in social attitudes, communication methods and product usage will occur? Much business planning is carried out from the perspective of frozen time. Imagine you are driving a car into the future. What will you see?

Stage 2: segmenting the market

Identifying need sets – the six questions
How, what, when, where, who, why? These six words form the basis of the majority of the questions it is possible to ask in the English language. Therefore, if you can define each answer arising from them in sufficient detail, they will detail the boundaries of any plan. For a segmentation study, the most important question is 'why?' This is because the answer arises directly from the fundamental values that drive desire

and create the want in the first instance. The buying process is an emotional proposition – you desire something and so you buy it.

The anatomy of desire

Our desires are filtered through our individual set of values. Values are deep-seated beliefs that, effectively, programme the brain. In other words, values determine how we think. If we think that one race is inherently superior to another, this may be part of our value system but we are unlikely to boast about it or confide it to a market researcher. Some values may be so deep-seated that we remain unaware of them and are unable to confide them to anyone, including ourselves. In addition, our self-image contains a perception of the person we aspire to be as well as the person we are. It is this aspirational individual who can easily surface in research. This individual generally believes in the right things. For example, he might not make purchases based on vanity, greed or sexual desire. The real individual may not be quite so well behaved.

Needs

Sometimes we want things because we need them, sometimes merely because someone else has something and we feel we deserve the same. In a complex social system, few products will sell on the basis of one clearly defined need. Usually a mixture will be involved and differences between the needs of customer segments will trace back to the manner in which these complex need sets are prioritised. For one buyer, the major need will be to minimise the cost while, for another, the major need will be to make a purchase perceived to be appropriate to his or her peer group. For a third buyer, the major need may be centred on an internally verified need, such as a connoisseur's belief in her ability to make a superior choice. Brands link into these needs by association and exploit the habituation process, i.e. we have not got time to make a choice so we go with what we already know. In every case the process is about what the product can do for the buyer, not about what it owns.

Why do they buy?
Describe where their desires come from:

- The desire to be healthy, well fed and watered and sexually attractive
- The need to be safe and protect and secure what we have
- The desire to be liked and accepted by others
- The desire to be respected for who we are and what we have acheived

Who buys our products?
Describes the customer.

What do they buy
Describes their product preferences.

Where and when do they buy?
Describes their shopping behaviour.

How do they buy?
Describes the process (by credit, for example).

The plan is complete when all six questions are answered satisfactorily.

Need set analysis needs to be cunning to tease out the underlying preferences. If funds are light or the the business is not large enough to withstand a large research budget, the task may have to be done intuitively. In either case the proof

of the pudding is in the eating. There is no need to be perfect.
If you make a significantly better job of it than your
competitors, the path is open for a dramatic gain. The trick is
always to be one step ahead of the competition. Sensible
competitor analysis will reveal how they slice up the market.
Can you beat them?

Completing the customer profile
Who are they?
It is useful to have a set of descriptions or profiles which can
check for preferences in terms of behaviour, motivation and
outlet choice. But beware, knowing that someone has plenty
of money does not imply they will always buy premium
products. They may well have plenty of money because they
are careful with it.

Where can they be found?
This includes geographic data, such as country, region and
area and urban, suburban and rural locations.

What are they like?
This explores demographic data, such as age, income, gender
and social class. The business-to-business scenario includes
size of business, type of industry, public or private
ownership and centralised or decentralized.

What do they value?
This covers psychographic information such as life stage
(child, adolescent, young adult, married with two children,
etc.) and lifestyle (how do they live).

Key drivers
Once you know who the buyers are and you have a good
understanding of the motivation that drives their purchase

behaviour, you can find out what they buy, where they go to get it, and lots more pertinent information.

Stage 3: screening segments

Some segments will be more attractive propositions than others. The segments should be screened and prioritised. The most attractive segments, which offer a good brand fit need to be selected, or at least prioritised, to receive the main effort. Some brands will niche on to selected segment(s) and others will have a wider appeal.

The customer profile map
The starting position is to map out the market segments you have identified. Figure 6 has five segments running vertically down the chart with preferences and known behaviours listed horizontally. The map should clearly describe the customer groupings and, if accurate, give a clear customer focus. Some datamining approaches (using huge computers to interrogate multiple databases) can provide 30,000 segments. However many you can find, you will only be able to effectively manage a number between five and nine. This is a human rather than a technical limitation. If you have more segments than you need, examine the potential for incorporating one or more together.

	New fans	Traditional fans	Corporates	Young	Women
Prime motivation	Excitement	Tribalism	Hospitality	Joy	Excitement
Description	ABC 1	C1C2	AB	ABC1C2	ABC1C2
	£21k–£30+k p.a.	To £29k p.a.	+£30k p.a.	–	–
Product preferences	Tickets	Tickets, shirts	Food	Football kit	Tickets
Purchase behaviour	Credit card	Cash	Credit card	–	?
Loyalty	Moderate	High	Low	Moderate	High
Buying process	Internet	Season ticket	Drinks	Xmas and birthday	
	Telephone	Stadium	Store	High street	
Channel split					
Stadium	48%	33%	1%	5%	13%
Merchandising	High	Low	Low	High	?
Media preference	Internet	Local press	Direct	Magazines	?
Growth	High	Stable	High	High	V. High
Contribution	55%	20%	3%	7	15
Size					

Figure 5 The customer profile map

The customer profile map in Figure 5 shows an indicative view of segmentation for a fictional football club. The female segment is growing but undefined. The other four segments offer clear, differentiated segments.

Identify what information you have available to design your segmentation and what is missing. How can you fill the gaps? Create your own segmentation map.

Stage 4: targeting segments

Determining the targeting policy depends upon the strategic approach. Do you view the business as a niche player focusing on one or two segments, or a generalist attempting to cover the whole market? If you decide to exit a segment, remember that it may create a vacuum that will be filled by someone else. Also, big segments tend to offer lower profits, but provide critical mass. For most businesses, the best answer is to target a strategic segment, i.e. one segment to receive the main effort together with one or more secondary targets. Some useful factors to consider when screening segments are outlined below.

Size The size of the opportunity. What is the total segment worth? What is its value in numbers of units of sale and the value of those sales?

Profitability How profitable is it?

Growth potential How deeply is the segment penetrated right now and, therefore, what is its likely rate of growth over the planning period?

Competitive strength How difficult a segment is it to compete in? Will we do battle with strong competitors?

Brand strength Is our brand respected and trusted in this market? What support has it had in terms of advertising spend? How well is it protected legally?

Distribution How good is the fit between the current distribution arrangements and this sector? Is there a good fit with our existing supply and value chain?

People Do we have the right mixture of people to make the most of the opportunity?

Money What are the entry or growth development costs? Can we afford them?

Timing Is this the right time to be making a strong move in this market? Are the economic and social trends favourable? What other signs and portents should we take account of?

Think about your focus. Describe the whole market you aim to serve (all the segments together). Which segment will be the main target of your effort this year? What segments will form secondary targets to receive some, but less, attention?

Summary

Your customer and prospect segmentation analysis is now in place and waiting to be aligned with the brand identity. You are now ready to move on to the industry analysis (competitors and channels).

Completing the audit

- Industry analysis: analysing competitors and channels to market
- Building a powerful platform for the brand plan

The market analysis is complete, with a strong brand identity in place and a rigorous customer evaluation and segmentation study completed. The next phase is an industry audit analysing competitors and marketing channels.

Choosing competitors

When antibacterial soap in dispensers reached consumers, it was positioned as a separate solution to existing soap. Existing competitors were bypassed and its delighted owners can now sell both types of soap. Sunny Delight achieved success by switching industry (or category as it is sometimes called) and moving into the chiller cabinets to compete against juices. Nicorette became a great success by switching category from doctors to consumers. In each case, the category switch moved the brands away from existing competition or into a new category without competitors. You are going to identify a competitive advantage, yet the choice of who to compete against is not necessarily obvious.

Industry analysis

Competitor analysis evaluates the competitors and potential competitors who could or might supply your customers. A new industry (group of sellers) can enter a market and spoil the party. Or you can move out. Cans replaced bottles as containers for beer and aircraft stole a large part of the shipping business. A new industry had discovered a new way of meeting needs in the marketplace. The pace of change is fast and wise businesses are alert to the comparative strengths of their potential as well as to actual competitors.

WHSmith is a communication store, which meets the desire to send and receive information. This desire is satisfied by newpapers, magazines and books (receiving information) and by pens, paper and writing materials (for sending information). This interpretation identifies other retailers dealing in these products, including supermarkets, as existing competitors. However, technology (e-mail, internet, interactive TV, etc) also meets the need to send and receive information. New competitors are feeding the existing market with substitute products.

Industry maps

Markets often divide into economy, middle and premium priced subsets, as depicted by the industry map in Figure 6.

The vertical price axis is a straightforward measurement of average prices and the horizontal axis takes a measurement of perceived quality (what the customers believe, not necessarily a demonstrable truth). The three star markers at the base of the map compete directly with one another, as do the five in the central slots. This leaves the top two premium brands to battle it out for the high price points.

Figure 6 An industry map correlating price and quality

The lowest of the stars represents a business with a clear quality and price advantage. It charges the lowest prices and is the best quality in its sector. The highest of the five central stars is overpriced and is likely to lose business. The business represented by the highest star appears overpriced compared to customers' perceptions and it stands to lose share.

Complete an industry map for your brand and interrogate it using the following questions as a starting point:

- Which brand holds the clearest price and quality advantage in your sector? What are the implications of this for your brand now and in the future?
- Which brand holds the weakest price and quality position? What opportunities does this open up for you?

Competitive advantage

Where, specifically, do your sources of competitive advantage lie? Take a couple of minutes to jot down your first thoughts.

Is your list painfully short, or worse still, empty? Sometimes the competitive advantages of a brand can be difficult to uncover, but for almost all brands they do exist. In fact, if they do not exist you are going out of business! Conversely, sometimes they are identified too readily and are later discovered to be insubstantial or untrue. 'Our people are our source of competitive edge' is a typical example. This statement may be true, but a wise manager would seek strong evidence before betting his or her career on it. If your list is long, revisit it and cross out any that now seem inadequate.

Teleology – the study of cause – provides a framework for a more thorough investigation. Four possible causes of competitive advantage arise:

1 *Organizational*: you are better organised than your competitors in some specific area or as an entity.
2 *Skill*: you have a skill advantage in one or more specific areas.
3 *Material*: you own, or have access to, superior physical and tangible resources. Your products and services are, in some way, superior.
4 *Soul*: an organisation that is aware of its purpose with clarity and precision rarely wastes time on non-essential tasks. Its is quite literally on a mission and the aura it grows around it is the stuff of legendary brands. This cause of competitive advantage is branding.

Competitive advantage lends itself to relational analysis ('better than, worse than'), rather than to precise measurement. It is likely, also, to be transient in the current fast-moving environment and so timing is invariably critical. A process is required that measures what advantages will occur and forecasts when to take advantage of them. This process begins with a comparative assessment of the key features of your product and service offer against your strategic competitors' offerings. The output of this comparative assessment can then be analysed in relation to the competitor analysis grid shown below.

We are very strong They are weak **Attack**	We are very strong They are very strong **Accept or re-engineer**
They are very strong We are weak **Take corrective action**	We are weak They are weak **Opportunity**

Figure 7

Competitor analysis grid
Each of the four boxes of the competitor analysis grid represents a directional policy: attack; opportunity; accept; correct. The attack option is self-explanatory, but there is a further opportunity where a weakness is shared. The first organisation to take positive steps to correct this weak area will probably score significant gains when the benefits become apparent to its customers. Accept indicates competitive parity – a drive for gains here is likely to be expensive. Correct indicates a weakness to be addressed, but one which is unlikely to quickly turn into an advantage.

Using a competitive advantage matrix

The next stage involves transferring the data you have amassed into a competitive advantage matrix (Figure 8). This will be your working document from which directional policy can be drawn.

Elements	Attack	Correct	Opportunity	Accept
Organisational				
Skill				
Material				
Brand				

Figure 8 The competitive advantage matrix

Against each of the first three causes of competitive advantage (organisational, skills and materials) list the key issues for your brand.

Compare the relative strength of each factor with a strategic competitor. Then, with reference to the competitor analysis grid record your responses within the appropriate boxes of the competitive advantage matrix. It should now be relatively simple to compile your competitive advantage matrix.

Brand equity

The fourth cause relates to brand equity (value). In many categories, consumers are often unable to recognise their favourite brands in blind tests (with the packaging removed), i.e. cola drinks, baked beans, whisky, yellow fats, razor blades, analgesics (pain relief).

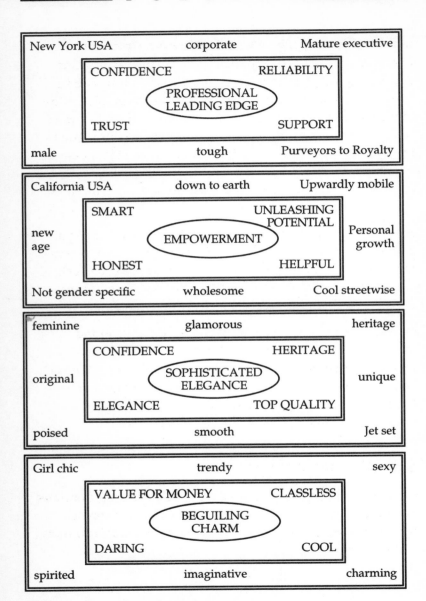

Figure 9 Brand identity interpretation

In principle, the equity of your brand is easy to establish. Compare the results of a market test with the brand name and packaging present, to an identical market test with the name and packaging removed. The difference in sales value of the two tests, grossed up to the full value of all the brand sales volume, equals the equity of the brand, i.e. its value to the business over and above the sales they would still have without it. This value arises from the intangible 'marketing brand equity', which the brand is able to lever to gain sales and margin, or both.

A good way to compare and contrast brands is to make pairs of brand maps to show comparative differences and to extract their strengths and weaknesses. Compare the matched sets of maps shown in Figure 9 and notice how quite small changes in the chosen words create distinctly different identities.

To compare and contrast brand equity, complete brand identity maps for your competitors' brands. Carry out a precise evaluation of your brand position relative to theirs. Look for attacking options and shared weaknesses and transfer significant differences on to the competitive advantage matrix.

Selecting the channel

Channel strategy is the last link in the 4C process. It examines the routes through which the company can make contact with its chosen markets (the groups of buyers of its products and services).

The value chain

The value chain is the total process that contributes towards
the final performance of the brand. It leads downstream
through the distribution outlets and communication activities
and out into the consumer world. It also leads backwards, to
the producers and suppliers sitting behind the brand. Value
flows down the chain but profits flow backwards, paying the
costs and profits of all concerned. The customers at the end of
the chain finance the whole operation when they buy the end
products and services. Therefore, wastage in the system,
especially excess stock, is paid for by the customers. A
competitor using a more effective value chain has a
competitive advantage. In a competitive environment, the
performance of the entire value chain is therefore a key
measure of success.

Downstream development
Where the brand enters the consumer domain there are likely
to be a number of options concerning the point of purchase
location. For example, high street stores, convenience stores
and out-of-town hypermarkets may find themselves
competing with the internet and direct selling methods. It is
important to look carefully at the options available and
decide where your focus should be. Consumers are not
always the direct customer. Some products form components
of a larger product.

Channel analysis

There are four layers to consider in analysing channels:

1 Environmental analysis
2 Power structure analysis
3 Economic analysis
4 Identity analysis

Environmental analysis

Socio-economic, political and technical changes may affect your various channels to market. The deregulation of the magazine market, for example, removed the monopoly of local newsagents and shifted sales towards the supermarkets.

Consider the socio-economic, political and technical changes that are likely to impact on your channels to market.

- Who are the likely winners/losers?
- What are the implications for your brand?

Power structure analysis

Below the surface, the big issue is power management. If your system is a bus, who is driving it? The driving seat of the bus is the best place to be. If you cannot be the driver, you must at least be near the front. Being thrown off the bus is disastrous. Power is usually the result of concentration of force. If five retail chains buy from 20 suppliers, the power structure will favour the retailers. If two suppliers supply 100 retailers the power structure will favour the suppliers.

Power is often used coercively and it is important to know some strategies that can influence the balance of power in your channel options.

1 The best strategy is a strong brand with a differentiated market and a clear and sought after point of difference.
2 A balance of in-house and out-sourced suppliers can reduce reliance on both by giving you the option to move your business towards or away from either.
3 A strong research and development function should ensure that you are at the forefront of new developments and not threatened by innovative new products.
4 Erect barriers to keep out new players. For example, direct communication links with partners using unique software will make it harder for new players to enter the fray.
5 Build strong relationships with high value channel partners and consumer segments to strenghten your position.

Consider the power relationships of each of your channel options:

> • Will the balance of power enable you to achieve your profit and sales targets or will you be brought into line with larger, more powerful partners?

Number crunch each channel to ensure that you know the current worth of each in terms of volume and value, profitability and net contribution.

> • Are there any hidden costs?
> • What are the growth prospects of each channel?

Identity analysis

Your brand needs to be in channels that complement its values rather than detract from them. This might entail some hard choices. A key point is the intensity of the channel. A high value brand will need a low intensity channel, i.e. relatively few outlets with premium standards of presentation and service. An economy brand, on the other hand, will require a heavy concentration of outlets and will survive with lower standards of service.

Consider how your channel options relate to the identity of your brand:

- Is the intensity of each channel appropriate to the value of your brand?
- What service levels are required for your brand?
- Do you need to supply high levels of training or supporting material? If so, you will need a stronger level of integration and cooperation between the two parties.
- Which channels will require key account teams to service them and which, if any, can cope with a lesser level of support?
- What are the relative costs to serve?

Each channel will probably be skewed, relative to your customer analysis. In other words, customer segments will be strongly represented in some channels and absent from others.

- What information do you have that will help you to understand the customer structure of each channel?

Finally draw a channel map similar to the one in Figure 10 (values are indicative only). Enter information on to the chart as shown.

Channel	Grocer	Convenience	High street	Wholesale
Environment	Grow	Grow	Grow	Fade
Power	Weak	Fair	Strong	Strong
ECONOMICS				
Size	200	71	78	82
Profit	14	24	16	12
Growth	High	Medium	Slow	Decline
Margin	6	34	21	15
Share	3	4	2	4
Loyalty	Weak	Strong	Strong	Fair
IDENTITY				
Brand fit	Strong	Weak	Strong	Weak
INTENSITY (outlets)	1000	250	301	72
Service	Good	Poor	Weak	Weak
SEGMENT (share)				
A	24	25	27	24
B	12	35	27	26
C	33	35	29	3

Figure 10 Channel map

Channel evaluation

Your final task is to decide which of your channel options are to be the primary outlets for the brand, which should be secondary and, possibly, which channels are unsuitable and should be exited.

Summary

You have carefully evaluated the channel options available, taking account of the big picture as well as the financial and brand identity issues. Power – the ability to push through with the brand objectives – has been an important consideration. Your 4C analysis is complete. The next stage is to pull the four separate pieces of work together into a coordinated and focused plan.

Positioning

- Preparing a situational report.
- Positioning your brand in the mind of its target audience.

Preparing a situational report

Congratulations on completing your 4C analysis. What you have prepared is a brand audit comprising:

- A brand identity statement revealing the key elements of the brand's anatomy and personality
- A customer map identifying your actual and potential customer base
- An industry map examining your chosen competitors and identifying potential points of difference
- A channel map examining your best placement for customer contact and sales

If you are involved with a major brand, it is likely that positioning and communications will be done in partnership with a creative agency. If so, this is the point to involve your account director. Agencies need to be involved to develop the strategy. Creative briefs developed by agencies are, in fact, positioning statements. Are you happy to pass the parcel onwards and devolve much of the responsibility to them? Working together would be preferred by most marketing directors. Rifts occur in most partnerships sooner or later, so decide on how you prefer to work (and who is working for whom.)

What will all this work look like when its finished?

Your challenge now is to transform the output of your analysis into a successful brand plan. This requires you to assemble all the relevant material you have collated and sift it carefully to shake out the less important data. What is left should provide you with a number of options that could potentially be taken forward. You will sift these options and identify the most appropriate for your purpose. At this point you will be able to see what your work is going to look like when it is finished. Once you know this, you will have translated your purpose into an outcome: you will have a strategy.

Creating a brand plan

A brand plan contains three elements:

1 The brand identity statement
2 A positioning statement
3 Growth vectors and drivers

Brand identity statement
This is the statement that you completed on Monday.
Remember that this represents the anatomy of your brand
and enables everyone who works with it to understand its
value and purpose. This permanent and unchanging
template ensures that your brand's core values, purpose and
consistency are maintained and protected.

Positioning statement
A positioning statement identifies the elements of the brand
to be positioned in the mind of the chosen customer segment
(the output of brand and customer analysis). In addition, it
uses a point of difference (from competitor analysis) and
identifies the best channel to market (from the channel
analysis). Unlike the brand identity, the positioning strategy
will need to be changed or adjusted periodically as customer
values and attitudes change.

Growth vectors and growth drivers
Growth vectors are the routes the brand will take, such as
entering new markets or developing new products and
services. Growth drivers are the elements of the marketing
mix that are most effective in creating delighted customers
and improving sales. For example, a vector would be the
decision to create an extension to the brand and a driver
might be the activities at the point of sale that are most
capable of building sales and profits. Together, they inform
decisions on business direction and the elements required to
deliver results.

Strategic thinking

The strategic decision process is supported by systematic analysis but requires a degree of intuition (and courage) to arrive at a differentiated and persuasive proposition.

To build your brand plan you will need to pull together all the data you collected from the 4C analysis and summarise it in a situational report (SitRep). This report will feed into the positioning statement. The remaining work will be to identify the growth vectors and drivers for your brand.

Creating a situational report

A SitRep is a working document. It contains a summary of your analysis that you can keep to hand and amend in the light of new information.

To pull together a SitRep for your brand you will need to answer the questions in Figure 11. Some people will be more than prepared to do this. Others, for a number of different reasons, may find that this more difficult. Don't worry, this is quite normal. If you are struggling, try using the techniques outlined on the following pages to liberate the required information.

Answer the questions set out in Figure 11.

1 What is my preferred product and brand focus?	2 Describe your general target market (all users and potential users)	3 Select a strategic competitor	4 Select a strategic channel (the one you plan to make the focus of your activities)
How will I leverage my competitive advantage? Where will the profit come from? Market growth % Share gains % Inflationary pricing % Cost saving %	Describe your strategic target (the segment of the market chosen for your main effort) Describe your secondary targets (any other segments chosen for a special effort)	(the one chosen for market share attack or strategic focus) State what attacking and defensive measures you plan to take	Select a secondary target
5 Competitive advantage	6 Assumptions	7 More research needed	8 Summary
What do you see as your main sources of competitive advantage?	What assumptions do you make about how the market is moving? What assumptions do you have about other factors (e.g. the economy) that are also likely to make an impact?	What facts or assumptions do you need to find out more about? Where can you find additional information to help you to develop your marketing plan?	Summarise below the main findings from your 4C analysis. What is the overall picture for your market?

Figure 11 Summarising the situational report

The following section notes some techniques to try if you are stuck.

The note party
Write down the equities of your brand using one note per equity. Do the same with the individual customer segments and then the various competitors and channels. The purpose

of this exercise is to experiment with a wide variety of combinations to identify the best options available to you. Assuming you organise the resulting notes into every possible combination and you have seven items in each box, you will be able to create 2,401 combinations. Many will be incongruent, but the promising ones will make an interesting story.

Summarise the answers into a story specifying your main points: How do you plan to grow? With what customer focus? Using what competitive advantage factor? Outputting through what channels? Work on what you have written until it is as compact as you can make it.

The dinner party technique
The dinner party. Imagine you have invited six celebrities to dinner. Get each team member to nominate one celebrity who they admire. Then the team members are invited to become that celebrity and, in this role, suggest some new ideas. Whilst in character, people may feel more comfortable expressing new views.

If you suspect some people are afraid to contribute fully, hand out white squares of paper and a pencil to everyone. Ask them to write down their ideas, anonymously, on to the paper and then to screw up the paper and throw it into an empty waste paper bin. Retrieve the bin and write all the ideas on to the grid.

When the ideas slow down
Study the analysis, discuss it with colleagues, have a bath, go for a walk, forget it and come back to it in a day or two. Reassuringly, marketing is a stochastic discipline, which means that there are no right answers (no company will ever

know if an alternative plan would have worked even better).

When you feel confident, return to summarising the SitRep.

Finalising your SitRep.
Your answers to the questions must be organised into a
coherent format. You may choose to lay them out as a series
of bullet points or write them out in report format. You now
have the basis for the current positioning of your brand and
its long-term development.

Selecting positional strategy

A positioning statement takes the key points from the SitRep
and arranges them to form the positional strategy of the
brand. All other strategies will flow from this central
position. The positional strategy should contain the
following:

- *What do we want to say?* The primary reason for
  buying your products and services that you will
  present to your audience. The source of
  differentiation. It needs to be presented from the
  receiver's point of view, i.e. as a benefit not a
  feature. It is the promise of beauty and
  sophistication, not a health and beauty product.
- *To whom?* The selected audience you will speak to:
  your strategic segment and possibly some
  secondary targets too.
- *Why?* Your proof. The substantiation to the
  proposition, derived from your principal competitive
  advantage. It can be something big, for example, a

major product advantage or something small if necessary. The skill is to create a scarce resource and make it attractive. The substantiation is often rational rather than emotional. The important point is that it must be different and attractive to the target audiences.

- *Against whom?* This is the competitor you plan to gain share from. Sometimes this is not the case. If the market is growing it would seem to be a redundant element. It is almost always useful to select a strategic competitor. It prevents the strategy from being too introverted and, besides, even the best general would be confounded if he or she was unable to discover the opponent. Today, most business activity is highly competitive. If not, then it is either a public service or very profitable indeed. In the second case, it is likely become highly competitive in the near future!

- *The brand essence* The core values of your brand give it credibility and must be accurately represented in the positioning statement. The brand's character, personality and tone of voice must be consistent with the message. In addition the brand's values and beliefs must be complemented and reinforced.

Write draft positioning statements for your brand following the format laid out above. Interrogate each one in turn by scoring it against the following questions on the basis of excellent (3 marks), reasonable (2 marks) and poor (1 mark). You may wish to add a weighting to each criteria.

1 Does it add value to the corporate plan?
2 Are our target markets valuable enough?
3 Is it consistent and coherent with our previous positioning?
4 Does it exploit competitor weakness?
5 How easy will it be to copy us?
6 Are there measures we can take to combat copying?
7 Can we afford it?
8 Have we measured it? Is it congruent with our forecast?
9 Is it distinctive, understandable, attractive and different?
10 Can we design contingencies?

Add up the scores to identify your best positioning statement.

Summary

You have prepared a situational report that summarises the main conclusions and decisions arising from your audit. The findings of the SitRep have been translated into a positioning statement. In addition, the discarded positioning options have all been measured against criteria that can be argued and justified amongst your team and to your senior management. Your brand identity statement and positioning statement will guide and lead the remaining decisions that need to be made.

Bringing the brand to life

- Operational planning
- Identify the most suitable growth vectors
- Align the drivers of business success.

Selecting growth vectors

So far, you have audited the brand and compiled the main findings in the SitRep. Using this data, you have faced the difficult task of identifying the brand positioning and essence. The directional policy of the brand is established: you know where you are going. What you need now is a route map to steer by.

You still have two sets of big decisions to make. The first set involves how to grow your brand. Growth is invariably the aim of business. The primary measurement of growth is Return on Capital Employed (ROCE). ROCE is how much you earn represented as a percentage of how much money you have put into the brand to create those earnings. ROCE is a function of the two secondary ratios: Return on Sales Ratio (ROSR) and the Asset Utilisation Ratio (AUR). Simplified, the business can only grow if it creates more sales or a better margin on the sales it is making, or both of these together.

There is a strictly limited choice and, therefore, it is well worth considering each one carefully. For example, you could decide to focus on new products or on entering new markets. Your best options for growth can be referred to as your growth vectors.

Having decided what route to take, the second set of decisions centres on changes you might want to make to the marketing mix. Broadly, the marketing mix divides into three key areas. The first is the goods and services you provide. Making these as well aligned as possible is your first task. The second area is logistics (the processes needed to get your goods and services to the right places at the right time and profitably). This requires tight management and successful partnerships. The third area is your communication with your target audience (and other public entities such as your owners, suppliers, etc.) about what you have to sell. Some changes in the mix will produce much better results than others. These can be called the growth drivers of the business. Your task is to find these and put them to work.

You have two tasks for today:

1 To identify the growth vectors for your brand
2 To establish the key growth drivers you need to work on
   to maximise the return on capital

Growth vectors

Let's examine each possibility in turn.

Improving profitability

There are two ways to improve profits: reduce the costs or put up the price.

Cut costs
Random cost-cutting invariably creates more, often hidden, costs. When looking for ways to improve profit margins the

focus should be on effectiveness, i.e. getting the job done properly and avoiding costly *firefighting* activities that go unnoticed in the formal accounts. Your channel analysis is useful here.

Look at your work on your supply chain. What changes can be made that will cut costs while maintaining efficiency?

- Can you reduce the number of suppliers?
- Can you tighten stock management?
- Can you strengthen the sales information system?
- Can you reduce paperwork by using the internet?

Put up prices

- *Value positioning*: putting up prices is the best way to make more money, provided the result is not a reduction in sales. Putting prices down is bad for branding and worse for profitability (unless it causes a very big increase in sales). Think about the problem as value rather than price. Could you offer:

1 Improved, perceived value at a higher price (a premium policy)?
2 More for the same price (can you add inexpensive extras or find someone else who will pay for them)?
3 Less value for a lower price (an economy policy)?

Revisit your segmentation and positioning:
- What possibilities exist for enhancing the range on offer to different segments?
- Would some segments benefit from improved value at somewhat higher prices?

- *Sensitivity analysis*: How sensitive are customers to price in your market? In some cases, an increase in price will result in a steep decline in sales, in others an increase can go unnoticed. It depends upon the customers. How familiar are they with current prices? To what extent are they prepared to shop around? There are often some segments which are not price sensitive even in a generally price sensitive market, for example younger, unmarried shoppers in supermarkets often have no idea what items cost.
- *Bundling*: it is not uncommon to find groups of products bundled together at a great overall price. Usually, there will be one or two that are substantially marked up in the overall price. Moreover, check the price points within a range – often some better sellers can be adjusted upwards and slower lines can be reduced in price.
- *Competitor reaction*: how will the competitors react to your actions? Work out what they will do and plan accordingly. If prices are to go up, wait until they put theirs up and follow behind. If prices are going down, be first and promote heavily.
- *Monitor Progress:* try to gauge the responses you get to price changes. Good customers tend to ask more of you, pushing up the cost-to-serve, while seemingly less valuable customers can be less demanding and therefore more profitable: know where your income stream is coming from.

Never treat a price as an isolated issue. Price is part or the overall value proposition. It is more about perception than reality. The cheapest product is rarely the best seller.

Improving sales

To improve sales you must either benefit from an improved market or take business away from your competitors.

Growing the market

- *Increasing usage*: the first place to look to increase usage is amongst your existing customers. Warm leads are better prospects than cold ones. A positive action would be to target existing, high worth customers with new offers. A defensive action could involve introducing an early warning system to monitor high worth customers and respond rapidly to problems.
  Understanding what a good customer is like enables you to look for more like them, rather than attracting price and deal-driven customers who will take the bargain and walk away.
- *Extending range*: Brands can be extended to incorporate new products and segments. The core values of the brand must not be compromised and must have the same meaning and relevance in the new segment. Secondly, unless it fits the distribution channel a new range can be expensive. Most brand extensions fail, so be careful. A real howler could seriously damage your brand.

- *Market growth*: If there is room to grow the current market and add new users, then the best process is to revisit the existing marketing mix and find better ways of doing what you are already doing. In particular, look for distribution gaps where you are not currently available.
- *New markets*: can be new geographic regions that you were previously unable to cover or newly identified segments within your existing coverage. Genuine innovation sometimes creates new markets. No one wanted anti-bacterial soap or energy drinks until someone invented them.

Growing market share

- *Buying rivals*: a good strategy, if you can afford it, might be to buy your competitor and thus take them out of the market. This avoids the potentially disastrous outcome of provoking a price war where everyone stands to be a net loser.
- *Alliances*: the internet is an example of the changing nature of competition. Website owners form alliances and deals, linking themselves to selected partners in a collaborative partnership. This creates networks and excludes non-members.
- *Beating rivals*: developing this strategy means deliberately setting out to persuade existing users to switch from their current supplier to you. In mature markets this is sometimes the only option.

Golden rules

- New customers will be non-users, buying for the first time or customers attracted away from competitors. Be clear about which of these types you are looking for.
- Wherever possible target influencers (e.g. family, friends, medical advisers etc), the people to whom new customers will turn for advice. Include existing satisfied customers in this if you can (remember the power of endorsement).
- Finally, make sure that your efforts to attract new custom do not favour prospects over loyal customers. Look for ways and means of communicating separately with existing and new customers to ensure that the separate messages do not cause conflict.

Selecting growth drivers

What elements of the marketing mix have the most impact on your business? What is it that really works for your customers? Some of the possibilities include: prices, product range, product quality, availability, speed of service, quality of service, 24 hour access, packaging, absence of packaging, the smell of the product, accessibility, reliability, information.

The trick, of course, is to know what will make the *most* difference. Many people in marketing have no idea. Or worse, they have their own, uninformed, opinion.

List all the marketing mix factors that you think make the most impact on your business and then rank the list from most to

least important. Add to the list your best estimate of how much
you spend on each. If the result shows the largest expenditure
at the top through to the least at the bottom, give yourself a pat
on the back. For ease of reference, display the results to map
your brand display curve, as shown in Figure 12.

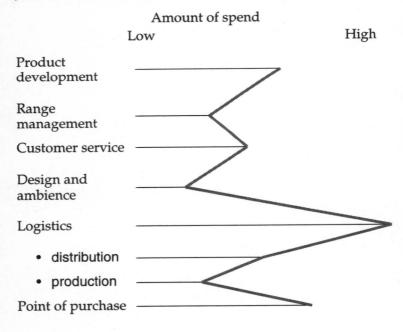

Figure 12 The brand spend display curve

The curve is also a good measurement of differentiation. The
design of your curve should show significant differences to
the curve of your competitors.

Brand tracking

Now find out what your customers think about the key drivers you identified. Transfer the meaningful data collected into action by testing it to verify its efficacy. If the change results in an improvement, keep it going and roll it out. If the test does not produce the result you wanted, try something else. Try out variations until you get the performance improvements you want. Brand tracking builds a set of qualitative and quantitive measurements to gain feedback on brand progress. A good brand tracker will need to be customised to suit the specifics of your business but it should contain three elements: exploration, development, evaluation.

A brand explorer investigates issues, such as occasion and reason for purchase, new ideas, how your goods are shopped and paid for and the effects of promotional activities. It will probably make use of omnibus research, dipsticks (rapid surveys), usage surveys, focus groups.

A brand developer experiments with the media mix, advertising, point of purchase and outlet choice and product changes. Normally, it involves the use of focus groups, depth interviews, workshops and observation experiments.

A brand evaluator tracks results and recommends changes. It may evaluate extensions, campaigns, trade and brand performance (financial). It will probably make use of omnibus research, particularly market share, sales audits and dipsticks in addition to observation.

Use your brand tracker to understand and make adjustments to the brand spend curve you completed earlier.

Design value into the brand

No business has infinite resources. Therefore, you will never
be able to solve every problem. It is necessary to make the
best possible use of scarce resources. Design the marketing
mix so that maximum resources are put into areas of high
perceived value to the customers (and/or consumers). Switch
costs away from areas that are less valued and into areas that
are. Figure 13 illustrates this point.

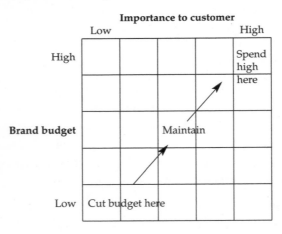

Figure 13 Brand alignment

Product management

Figure 14 is a useful format to evaluate products. High
turnover, low contribution products are usually 'traffic
builders', pulling custom through the system. 'Top
performers' deliver volume and profit and should receive top
billing. 'Problems' are highlighted for attention.

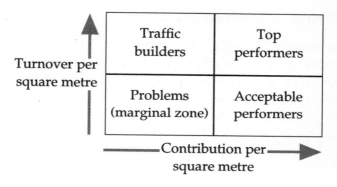

Figure 14 Product evaluator

Complete a product evaluator for your product range:

- Are the 'top performers' receiving the attention they deserve?
- If you have 'problem' products, how can they be adjusted to improve their performance? Should they be retired and the customers migrated away to other products?

Logistics management

Logistics is a crucial element in modern marketing. If the supply channel is inadequate, staff will be unable to deliver good customer service. If they do not have appropriate tools, resources and products they cannot do the job.

Customer service

Good customer service is rare and, therefore, differentiating.
Recruit people who like your brand and who are like the
brand and you will be a long way towards achieving this
objective.

> Virgin employes young, streetwise people.
> Waterstones employ people who love books

All staff should know the importance of keeping good
customers. Make sure they know the marketing cost of
gaining new custom (customer acquisition cost). Service
quality often revolves around a moment of truth during the
service transaction, during which customers are gained or
lost forever.

> A well known marketer, speaks movingly of when his
> father died. The hospital (contrary to the more common
> anecdotes in the press) treated his father and family
> with great respect and professionalism. Following the
> inevitable ending the hospital handed over his fathers
> belongings: in a bin liner. Look for moments of truth.
> Look out for bin liners.

Five golden rules for great customer service

1 Structure the business around customer value and manage customers for profit, not volume.
2 The first customer contact should be the best point of contact. Put your best people in contact with your customers, not the worst.
3 Always keep your promises.
4 Centralise service to single points of contact.
5 Make sure your star customers get star service.

Summary

The brand is moving into alignment with its aspirations, its audience and its marketing mix. We know now where it is going and how it is going to get there. It has yet to speak and that is what we will be going at next.

When the brand speaks

Preparing the brand messages

Before diving into the field of marketing communications we can examine communication and consider Marshal McLuhan's famous diktat: 'The medium is the message'. You progress to how to utilise communications to build brand equity. Then we shall cover media and the tools that can be used to promote your brand and incentivise your customers.

What is communication?

> The ability to communicate with one another more effectively than any other animal is the essence of being human. Because we have language we can think . . . or is it the other way around?

Understanding the process of communication involves the mind analysing itself. It is unsurprising that progress has been slow. It is useful to view communication from the perspective of the response, rather than the output, because it is not the performance of the communicator that matters but the results achieved. Feedback is the essence of the process. If a communication produces the right response, all is well. If not, the process is repeated and, if necessary, varied until it does.

Understanding how advertising works is as complex as understanding why a novel is good or bad. Fortunately, this is not an imperative in brand management because your task is to measure its output: its level of persuasiveness.

The medium and the message

The medium is the message. Of course this is true. They co-exist within a communication: the medium is the context of a message and the message is the content. Non-verbal signals (body language) provide a context for communication. They are more important than words because the meanings of words are verified by the context in which they are received.

Try telling someone you hate them while smiling warmly. Then tell them you love them with a snarl. See?

It follows that brand messages need to be positioned correctly for context and content. Lucozade, originally, was positioned as a drink to make sick people healthy. Later it was repositioned as a fitness drink to help healthy people stay healthy. It remains a health drink, but the message has been re-framed. The positive context works better because health protection and well-being fit our current culture more than health recovery.

A successful advertisement compared Christmas trees to cut flowers. The advertisement pointed out that the deteriotation of both commences when they are cut and that the advertised Christmas trees were always sold on the day they were cut. This advertisment caught customers' attention because of the association and because it was relevant (consumers only take notice of Christmas tree commercials when they want one, i.e. at Christmas) . The result was measurable both in sales of the product (short term effect) and in the brand equities of quality and service (long term effect).

Sometimes advertising is too clever and customers fail to link the advertisement to the product. If the audience love your advertisement, are they transferring this emotion to your brand? The sales figures will tell you the answer.

Your task in relation to communication boils down to: 'What do we want to say, with what, to whom?' The work you have already completed on positioning your brand has prepared you well for this.

Building brand equity

Effective communication builds the equity of your brand. To achieve this, powerful objectives, strategies and tactics need to be determined.

Communication objectives

Communication objectives aim to build awareness, understanding and perception of the brand. They create influence. They should inform changing attitudes and preferences. Examples can be to:

- Increase sales volume
- Persuade customers to try out the product
- Increase weight or frequency of purchase
- Build brand loyalty
- Widen product/service usage
- Create interest in the brand
- Develop awareness and preference towards the brand
- Direct attention away from price increases or other bad news

- Win preference down the trade channel
- Define user differences to build sales range

Strictly speaking, sales gains are not a communication objective but a marketing objective (communication does not earn money – it spends it). In actuality, this is unrealistic. Of course you will judge your promotional results against sales performance. If the equity of your brand grows, it will be reflected in increased sales.

Choose two or three of the communication objectives listed above and turn them into precise, measureable outputs for your brand, for example, 'By 31 March, our top ten clients will make us their preferred supplier and order 30 per cent more than 31 March last year.'

With clear objectives you can describe precise outputs that can be measured and tracked. The list below specifies the key result areas.

Evaluating advertising:

- Is it relevant to its audience?
- Does it specifically attract sales?
- Does it build brand values?
- Is it memorable, distinctive and on strategy?
- Is it positive and action oriented?

Communications strategy

An effective communications strategy will cover the following areas:

1 Brand essence

2 Brand positioning
3 Integration
4 Creative treatment
5 Selection of media and tools
6 Push and pull strategies
7 Burst and drip advertising

Brand essence and positioning
Your brand essence and positioning are in place. They will appear in the copy strategy that you will develop shortly. Your copy strategy will be used to direct operations.

Integration
A key consideration must be how to ensure that messages are integrated to deliver a sufficient degree of coherence. Failure here can result in your target audience reeiving messages that are contradictory and confusing.

Creative treatment
The essence of the creative treatment is in your positioning statement. This will need to be translated into a briefing document.

Selection of media and tools
Media and tool selection is covered in the next section.

Push and pull strategies
A major strategic consideration is the promotion of the brand identity and reputation of the business. Strategies to attract customers or consumers are often called pull strategies. These centre on the pulling power of the brand, developed by talking to customers and consumers. Strategies to win distribution and trade battles are sometimes called push strategies. These focus on the drive down the trade channels

through to the point of purchase. You need both.

Burst and drip advertising

You will need to decide whether you are going to hit hard by squeezing a large proportion of budget into a short period of time or whether you will space your campaign out over a longer period. The most common approach is to use bursts of intense advertising at peak periods with a much lower intensity of effort throughout the remainder of the planned period (burst and drip).

Tactical development

This work is normally carried out by an advertising agency. The information covered in this section provides you with an overview of the creative techniques they may employ.

This is the fun part of marketing communications. It involves devices such as logos and signatures, characters like Lara Croft, memorable slogans, for example, 'A Mars a day helps you work rest and play' and clever packaging like the special jars and bottles of Bovril and Heinz Salad Cream. Inspirational use of these devices can create a strong presence down the trade channels as well as in promotional work.

The message you design needs to persuade your audience, not yourself. The required outcome is to persuade your target audience to behave the way that you want them to. Agencies employ a wide range of techniques to ensure that your message is powerfully received. Some of the most common are outlined below.

Metaphors and metonymy

A metaphor is a story that illustrates a point. Stories are

frequently used in advertising to engage attention.
Metonymy utilises one aspect of an item to emphasise the
whole. The 'Cream of Boddingtons' campaign is an excellent
example of this.

Memorability
Memorability is essential. Repetition is memorable. Being
first is memorable. Who was the first person to climb Mount
Everest? Who was the second?

Golden rule
Awareness of a brand is useless in itself. The
awareness needs to be linked to relevance and
preference. Brands need to progress to a customer's
shopping list.

Word power
Frost damage results from broken freezer bags, but
describing frost damage as Freezer Burn has sold many more
bags. Acid rain probably won more research funds than
pollution ever did.

Endorsement
A famous German advertisement compared a group of grafitti
sprayers to a dog peeing up a wall. The young audience
roared with laughter – the graffiti artists were laughed at by
their peer group and the incidence of graffiti damage shrank.
Successful advertising needs powerful endorsement because
it supplies a reason to believe. Brands utilise endorsement to
link themselves to believable sources and become
endorsements themselves for their sub-brands. In some
countries, Nestlé sells KitKat and in others KitKat sells Nestlé.

Positive thinking and talking
A traditional rule of advertising is to avoid negative statements.

In your mind's eye picture a cuddly toy. Now picture not a cuddly toy. Can you do that? If you recalled a picture of another cuddly toy you have got the point. Negatives are language constructs with no tangible reality and so they are hard to conceptualise. Consequently, advertising your brand as not poisonous will associate it with poison in the mind of your target audience.

Copy strategy and briefing

This document guides policy and protects the equity of the brand, ensuring long-term consistency. It also keeps campaign work on strategy. Use it to make clear what you want, leaving enough room for creativity to flourish. Avoid jargon and consultant speak – it gets in the way of communication. Much poor advertising occurs because clients fail to communicate their wants clearly. Reject any creative work which fails to conform to the plan.

A well-written copy strategy will contain the following elements:

- *Brand integrity*: the key characteristics of the brand. This section will specify the brand anatomy, its personality and essence. Your brand identity statement has done this job already. Make sure that intellectual property is legally protected and that there is clarity about who owns what.

- *Background*: illustrate previous work that has been done. Give enough background to make it clear where the brand has come from.
- *Brand Positioning*: use the statement that you have already prepared.
- *What is the advertising hoping to achieve?*: turn your objectives into output, i.e. what you expect to happen as a result of the communication campaign. Spell it out.
- *The target markets*: write a description of your target audience in plain but warm words. You need to like them to sell to them. Avoid words like contemporary and relevant as in 'Making the brand contemporary and relevant!' Say, 'We need to demonstrate that the brand is up to date and in touch with its audience.' Remember, your audience may include decision makers, influencers and buyers, in addition to end users.
  Be prepared to make sacrifices, i.e. deliberately giving up some consumer opportunities in order to be compelling to the remainder. The choice lies between taking a broad or a narrow position. A broad position may lead you to miss completely.
- *The proof*: this is your endorsement or substantiation – the proof that what you are saying is true. This is drawn from your positioning statement.
- *Tone of voice*: this is drawn from your brand identity statement.

Write a copy strategy for your brand, following the format shown above.

Selecting media and tools

A useful distinction between communication methods
Communication can be directed towards individuals as in
direct marketing or towards groups of individuals as in
advertising. The first is very personal (and potentially
intrusive if you get it wrong). The second is much more likely
to create discussion (word of mouth in the jargon). The two
communication methods are not in competition because they
produce entirely different results. One-to-many
communication can make you famous whereas one-to-one
builds relationships. The table below lists some of the options
available.

Media	Tools
Advertising	Sales promotion and sampling
• Display and classified	Merchandising and packaging
• Terrestrial television	Customer service
• Satellite and cable	Public relations
• Video	Direct marketing
• Press, print	Personal selling
• Cinema	Exhibitions, demonstrations, events
• Outdoor	Sponsorship
• Radio	Product placement
• Cyberspace	Relationship marketing
• Ambient	Guerrila marketing

Media buying and advertising

Buying media is best left to specialists When choosing
advertising and media agencies a good place to start is the

Incorporated Society of British Advertisers (ISBA) who will advise on best practice and agency selection.

Selecting tools

There are a variety of tools available to you.

Sales promotion
Sales promotion is a skill in its own right, offering as much scope for ingenuity and brand development as advertising. Furthermore, the £8 billion UK spend far exceeds all the money spent on advertising. Substantial investment here needs to be supported by a specialist agency. Sales promotion splits into four types:

1 *Price promotions*: common examples are 'cash back' and 'no VAT'.
2 *Value promotions*: these include such things as larger packs and consumer games and competitions.
3 *Now or later* : this can be applied to both price and value promotions. The offer can be given immediately at purchase or delayed by the means of coupon collection, etc. Levels of offer redemption can be an unknown quantity in delayed promotions and this can be catastrophic. Sales promotion disasters fill the black museums of marketing.

Viral
Viral marketing is a term coined to describe the success of Hotmail in advertising its free service on its e-mail banner. This action was largely responsible for 12 million new customers. This is because an e-mail

message can be exponential. In other words, e-mail users gossip by posting items attachments to one another. One young lady sent a saucy e-mail to her boyfriend who promptly copied in his friends. This un-gentlemanly act reportedly led to 10 million readers within a number of days.

Buzz
Similar to viral but outside the internet. Using clever ideas that will spread by word of mouth.

4 *Sales promotion strategy*: 'What do you want to achieve, with what?' is the question that underpins effective sales promotions. What outcome will be linked to what mechanic (i.e. competition, special offer)? There is no limit to the creative cunning that can be used.

Reggie the Bath Duck is an example of a mechanic employed by a hotel chain. He inhabited guests' bathrooms and an accompanying text invited guests to float him in the bath or send him free of charge to a friend or a child. The objective, to build referrals from established guests, was a great success.

A key to building value into sales promotions is the creative use of partnerships. A promotional specialist might buy surplus tickets from an airline at a low price and sell them on to a marketer who produces an offer that requires the winner to travel free but with a friend. Of course the friend must pay the standard price and so the cost of the flight is recovered. Everyone wins.

Public relations

Public Relations (PR) specialists play a vital role in many marketing operations. Marketing PR is a term sometimes used to identify PR activities that are built into the marketing plan.

> The announcement by Heinz that they might have to remove Salad Cream from their list created an outpouring of love for the brand. This is marketing PR in action.

Design agencies

Design has an important role to play in identity management, packaging and elsewhere. For many brands, design is as important as advertising. For example, a retail store is by far the most important advertising message from the retailer. If the shopping environment and experience is poor they fail.

Personal selling

Skilled personal selling, when backed by promotional material, is far more effective for a small target audience than advertising can ever be. It is dependent, however, on the ability and skills of the salesperson. In this instance, recruitment and training enter the marketing mix.

A marketing campaign might be designed as follows:

- *Leader (first wave)*: advertise nationally on local radio to build awareness.
- *Middle (second wave)*: sales promotion to provide added incentives.
- *End (final wave)*: direct mail to build loyalty.

Review the media and marketing tools covered above and decide how the promotional campaign for your brand should be structured.

Timetable and budget

The only logical approach is to decide what you need to achieve and whether the result will be a justifiable return on the investment.

Controls and contingency

It makes sense to keep some funds in reserve to reinforce success. Controls should include variance analysis against the budget. Individual agencies should be tasked with monitoring their own performances, although the use of a specialist as a third-party analyst ensures objectivity. Sales uplifts should be included. Put them in a separate section because they are influenced by circumstances detached from this plan.

Focus groups, tracking studies (more about these tomorrow) and recall tests can be used. Most importantly, if your objectives are specific and measurable it will be possible to monitor and evaluate them effectively.

Summary

The world of marketing communications is vast, with hosts of specialists and terrifying costs. This chapter has considered the most important issues involved, i.e. the messages the brand needs to send out to its audience and the media and tools that can be used to carry them.

Managing the plan

- Review of the process
- Preparing, managing and presenting the plan
- Concluding thoughts

Completing the plan

You are now at the final stage of the brand planning process – pulling your brand plan together. Once you have a finalised brand plan, you need to move from concept to action by completing a project plan. You may need to present your plan to senior managers and so today you shall cover a suggested format for this purpose. Finally, you will need to finalise tracking procedures to measure results and make changes.

Completing your brand plan

By now, the key elements established by your analysis should have directed you towards a clear identity and positioning for your brand. Over the last two days you have worked through possible vector strategies, hopefully making some selections, and pinpointed the key issues driving your product, logistic and communication plans. Your decisions concerning the growth drivers and vectors for your brand, made in the context of your brand identity and positioning, comprise your brand plan. The complete process is summarised in Figure 18.

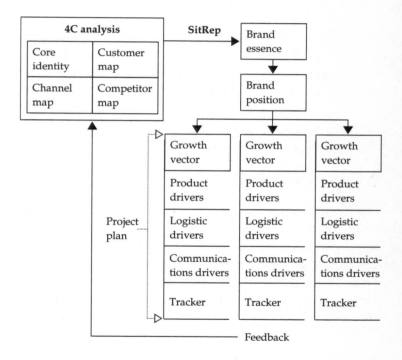

Figure 18 The planning process

Remember, the brand identity must be a consistent beacon throughout your plan. Your brand must be represented in harmony with its identity in everything you do, from defining your growth strategies to point of sale. In other words, the brand must behave how you designed it to.

The positioning of your brand is the focus of the plan. This is what the brand says when it speaks. Just as with good literature, your brand's dialogue must always be true to character. If it was Boddingtons it would say 'creamy' in an amusing, Mancunian manner. If it was Nike it would be living for sport and behaving a touch dangerously. Your brand's positioning must inform all three growth drivers: products and services, logistics and communications.

> If Rolls Royce is positioned as the ultimate car, its product specification and price will be premium, its channels will be exclusive and will deliver outstanding service and its communications will be limited to a selected, exclusive media.

The growth vectors are your chosen growth strategies, selected from all the possible routes. Avoid choosing dozens. Two will be a challenge for most brands.

The growth drivers in your plan are the focal points of your marketing mix.

Products

For each growth vector you need to map out a product plan over 12 months, covering financial forecasts, product specifications, packaging and a pricing plan. Your sales forecast should be based on historical data in relation to an average month. Remember to smooth out the bumps that were the result of one-off events. Adjust the results to take account of your forecast for the next year's trading, including predicted consumer spending, inflation and predicted changes in your business sector, especially price increases. Then adjust the result for seasonal changes, mirroring the historical record from last year. Finally, add your growth projection. Be bold but not crazy. Rampaging growth is extremely hard to manage.

Logistics

You will need to consider logistics in relation to your products, distribution and channels and quality. Using your product plan, make certain that you can make or buy the necessary components required to meet your product plan. In other words, can you get the right products to the right people at the right price, place and time? Adjust the product plan only if you are certain that the logistics are unattainable. Remember that quality is a vital equity and your customers' perception of the quality of your brand must be protected at all times. Refer to your channel analysis from Tuesday.

Communications

Your copy strategy for your brand specifies what the brand will say, to whom and with what proof. You will need to make your decisions about what media and tools to use. Use either advertising, sponsorship, PR or the sales team, backed with appropriate literature, to start the campaign. Use

promotional tools, such as sales promotions to support the
campaign later on and consider direct approaches to build
and reinforce loyalty towards the end. Seasonality will be a
vital factor in timing the campaign to support the major sales
drives. Use bursts of activity at key periods and space some
spending out over the remaining time as reminders. If a big
budget is to be spent, make certain that professional help is
used. Even if you are spending a small budget, remember
that the media world is a jungle and think twice about
entering without a guide.

Integration

The three pieces of work, which selected the drivers of the
brand strategy (Product, Logistical and Communication
drivers), should be mapped out onto a calendar and carefully
matched to ensure that the product plan is delivered by the
logistics and communication plans. Finally, all of it should
support and deliver the brand's positioning.

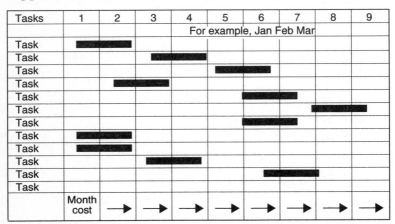

Figure 19 The Gantt chart

Named after its creator, the Gantt chart is a good way to chart the product, logistic and communication tasks. Make a list of the tasks down the left-hand side and mark the calandar section with a line indicating the completion time for each task. For big brands, the three components will need separate charts. The various tasks can be costed downwards on the calandar, giving a monthly total expenditure that can be added up to establish the full year's expenditure.

Creating a formal Plan

The Gantt chart and diary objectives form your working documents. However you will probably need to create a formal document for presentation to senior management. Formal marketing plans have a tendency to make a grand entrance and a mouse-like exit. Cupboards everywhere are full of them. Workable planning lies in the processes explained in this book. If you need a formal plan to present to the bank or the board keep it simple following the format below:

Introduction
1 Objectives
2 Strategy
3 Elements (the mix)
4 Programme
5 Budget (cost of plan and outcome)
6 Responsibility
7 Controls
Summary

Finally, make sure you have complied with company procedures and that lead times are taken fully into account. Go back through your arguments. Have you made a strong case? What are the key points? Concentrate on the strongest two or three points and justify them with well thought out arguments.

Review of the marketing planning process

The work you have completed today has produced a project plan and a formal presentation document with which you are well armed to win the commitment and resources you need to live your ideas. You have now completed the full planning process and have created a powerful plan for your brand. Congratulations!

Summary

Quality
Consistancy and quality are the hallmark of great brands. A Mars Bar is always a Mars Bar. It does not vary in quality, the taste is consistantly the same. Quality is relative and perceived. Relative because it is relatively better than its competitors and perceived because its quality resides in the perception of its consumers. It is only great quality if they believe it. Branding cannot offer protection for shoddy work.

What if it all goes wrong?
A brand is like a bubble. It can grow and become all encompassing but it can also burst. There is evidence to suggest that the best response, if things go wrong, is to own up. The public will forgive and forget errors but not

mendacity. For many years, Marks & Spencer made a virtue out of mistakes when they inevitably occured. A faulty product would be massively advertised. 'It is no good! Send it back for a full refund, our apologies and all sorts of goodies!' The results were invariably brand-reinforcing and very positive. What a great company! Brands can, and do, recover from disaster.

What never to do

> ## How to kill brands dead
> - Bring out innumerable line extensions that do not fit the brand and which the consumers do not want
> - Cut prices and devalue them, stripping out value and profit for reinvestment
> - Bring in a brand manager with little or no experience and watch him or her change everything just for the sake of it, before leaving to get another job
> - Focus everything on this month's performance and to hell with the longer run
> - Spend a fortune on research and then run the same boring advertisements as everyone else
> - Make a plan that faithfully records the past and ignores what might happen next
> - Do nothing until you have run some focus groups and then do everything they say

Think for yourself
Marketing today is less about communicating effectively and more about developing good ideas that stand out from the incessant noise of saturation broadcasting, tedious direct mail

and intrusive telephone calls. The best way to build customer relations is by being interesting enough to attract their attention.

Playing a different tune

Every business segment or category has rules. These rules are often unspoken, for example, serious newspapers are broadsheet and popular ones tabloid. If they are valued by your customers, then breaking them is risky. Many of the big gains in business, however, come from ignoring these rules.

Good luck!